COMIC TIMING

COMIC TIMING

Holly Pester

GRANTA

Granta Publications, 12 Addison Avenue, London W11 4QR

First published in Great Britain by Granta Poetry, 2021

A CIP catalogue record for this book is available from
the British Library.

10 9 8 7 6 5 4 3 2 1

ISBN 978 1 78378 686 2
eISBN 978 1 78378 687 9

Typeset in Minion by Hamish Ironside

Printed and bound in Great Britain by T J Books, Padstow

For Sam and Zara

CONTENTS

ACT 3

ACT 4

ACT 1

Heavy in me

shall I shrink in the water or spin (*ah*) here is love and here is death (*eh*) it is fare in brine (*ah*) shall I breathe it (*ah*) shall I drink (*ah*) or submerge (*eh*) shall I sweat (*eh*) if I twist in the water I glimmer (*eh*) shall I hang by the jaw in water and twist like a bug shall I kick (*ah*) shall I thicken in a bottle or submerge (*ah*) crawl back to life and breathe (*ah*) bring up sick between fingers link breath to brine shall I bathe or swell shall I crawl into my neck and link breath to brine (*ah*) shall I breathe (*eh*) or crawl back (*ah*) into my neck

LONG

To those who began the year being
bullied, violently shaken
Who know beginnings
felt unstoppable
Yes, longer
Not to be corseted, or sung manipulated
Shout at me the time
Get into me the time
It's 2000 and 19
Vapours start again
The fireworks are from yesterday
Purple murderers green ones
A head pops off
I'm unsure of the time
But it lasts
A memory should be better
Practised
But it's over
To those who began the year being
bullied, corseted, violently shaken
May they know all beginnings
unrepeated unrehearsed
Yes, longer

THIRTY-SIX

you must be –
alive – when looking dead
                Marilyn Monroe

Stories like starting points.
Beata Beatrix is on the mantelpiece.
She is steady and blissful with a bowed neck.
Her neck is too long but must be to convey the stretch
of death into life
and the narrative discontinuity that death follows life.
I am stupid for getting into debt paying rent.
The young woman with the stretched neck is long gone
but still going.
Today I got up.
I was 36 for too long and for one more week.
The day is dragging on the time to come.
I am stupid in a room that I owe for.
I could stay here forever.
I am bowing, indebted but had no choice;
wages and rent conspired without me.
Long ago a living space naturalised
tenant debt to landlord.
I bear a room and time.
Who can read and write in here?
The room will change soon.
This is the monument and tide of a life.
At what point is this a life?
I get older and have lesser, my debt to the room is morer.
I work harder but am lazier, tireder and there is more to do.
The things to do are bigger and less material.
I cannot be bound or unbound
so I am transfixed to heartbeat and bowing.

This is a kind of writing heritage.

The room's commitments make me static.

But I forgive myself for lapsing, for turning around to lie down.

Granddad was an artist who died at 36.

His self-portrait is brutishly Modern, holding up time with paint.

An era and a look locked into his career that died with him.

His paintings hang, still.

Marilyn Monroe was an actress who died at 36 and continuously.

Something about the time and the age of that act became impossible.

She couldn't bear it.

Something about the contract she was in, lapsed.

She had already created a past.

A means to alienate act from time.

It is funny how sexy she was and how that was the hairstyle all of our grandmas had.

That's lucky but I am worried.

I am on the verge of an age I haven't accounted for and cannot afford.

I am in a contract that makes me nervous, ideas are building up.

I service my work with accommodation.

Rent is an attribute of work and a profit of poetry.

This is a kind of wage heritage.

There is no way to leap like a flea into security other than marriage or a great big prize.

How else do I cut myself off?

I should have a look and lie down.

I live in the room abstractly.

I lie in the room fundamentally.

I work but I owe.

Sleeping is on the to-do list.

There is borrowing within the borrowing and death inside the life.

There is guilt on the threshold and ever since.

SOME LIKE IT HOT

   she had a good night and is not going back
I've got extra ordinary things to do
I'm on my way to the shop
   I want today
there is time for you tomorrow night or tomorrow morning
there is never a global night
I want you at work and you want to work
I don't think you want me
   I'm going back on you
you can come with me tomorrow
there is only greatness at night
but you want to go to the shop
   get me a little room
the problems of the family will meet me
get the kids to come and pick me up
I'll go to the shop for something
I'll pick you
   I was a couple of hours late and you picked a coffee
   I'm not going back out
you've got a room and you'll have a good night
   I want time
   I want you at night
you have greatness at night
   you were coming to pick up the boys
   I waited in a little town
   I'll be here when you get back
I am leaving on Sunday
I want a couple more hours of sleep
   We could go to tomorrow in holy rounds
I have a couple of strange hours
and not much to worry about too

CALL IN SICK

my commute is not bad
it is alive and turny
nothing is that hard I
will
look at other routes
I am
about to stack a tower
on someone else's route
my commute
is easy I'm wearing
it I've seen them I can't
believe you can buy
them very conventional
and everyone looks
outside throughout
who
is secure apart
from the makers of travel
I'm wearing
anything not to
look like
what married women
go to sleep in
embalmed
evacuees and weavers lie
in the tower
of obscenities I'm wearing
them I came
all the way here
little high
street intensely

HISTORICAL BED SORES

some women cup their breasts and women without breasts chirp at
the thought

women hold their babies up to the light and the women without
babies weep at the thought

women with tears in their eyes with gas in their mouth can pose with
tigers in the bath

tigerless women check the number of breasts their childless heads
their breastless chests

their sore bone rectangular, triangular

armless kids climbed inside a clock

the women with no breasts with red gruesome hair are kin

prepare bowls of hot gum

in our bellies

we have clowns and bugs

we have mock breasts and bellies like bowls of hot gum

frig the dried blue men

a soup for my sister a new earhole where her wound is a light

the women without babies sing into cat bellies

we hunt for sliced up income

for mamma's dark red underwear

strong girls breathing in rivers

drinking out of each other   speaking out of each others' backs

sing for our empty friend

some river bellies some ocean some singular bump

health custard

bomb shoes

who killed our cave? who let out our weal?

a cave for my baby

a rubber ball full of honey

without babies we chirp into caves

drinking a pool of tomato pips and the last strings of egg

delicious forever

find a cave for my injured friend

DOCTOR!

in the middle of an unspiritual seizure
to the doctor I am concerned
about my flushes and blood pressure
is it a small note on my cheek forever?
he was as amazed as cardiac
These freaks you're holding
A child and A child grating my arms
What do you call them?
Scrat and Fend

ABORTED

Like history this sliced up worm carries on in both directions
I know thee, I have found thee, & I will not let thee go

They dug and buried
arrests were made

Giving birth by a hedgerow I ask the hedgerow what it feels
like to be broken into

It was verses we should've sung
bring back my
I doubled up

Is there a dead bird in you?
– no
　　　You're a strike-through line
dived over your sitter to the next incur

Ask me. Do I end here. I fail. I drink a foot. I ask the wall
What plot did you sneak
to improve the noun for staff?
to slur a rebel's speech

livers split　out pours solution
– a worm
　　　　ask it

ODD KILL

Days develop sideways, I am interested in life. It lives and I remain interested. But what in the complex droop of life is in my interests? Not life. Not its interesting weeds.

Much of 'human life' is not in my interest. Not like a mouse is very much in its cage and a pound is absolutely in the bill. There is a centre that is not recreation. But my interests live in me and it is in my interests to live. My interests have aims, a singular aim is to live but they want more. They want to be saucy.

Once my saucy, bulking, hardened, skin-on interests were satisfied by living I went up to them and found inside a sense of self. Small and slaughtery, like an office or canned forest. All of a shorted voice began.

An invoice. Then my sense of self was a blatant orange ball, starting to live.

The plan to live invites itself in. Especially having learnt to say 'in and of itself'. Convictions fail, I am all by my self. Sitting in the beginning of linen. The big linen aims for life are full of conviction and passionate content that are difficult. All craft and yearning, a big tent with a sleeping bag in it. The bag represents the content of my conviction in the living, its material is in my interest. I am interested above all in livers.

The bag is passion and grows bigger than the tent. My 'sense of self' goes hugely odd but is still in my interest, firmly like a skull, unbudgeable. Nothing has died yet but that's coming, as the interesting bag of passion grows livers.

Because living is coming into existence, passion is coming to life, killing is growing conviction. A killing conviction is life's content. Life is in my interest, along with tents and dopamine.

As a life dies it's interesting because that's when it can accommodate existence. It is in my interests, alongside the mouse, to enjoy existing. It is in my interest for the content of my conviction to be a kill. I think my interests are a cage.

At least in a cage with a packet of livers I am real, I have arbitrariness, I am happy with that to be in the interests of my life. On a strip of linen, a sense of self is sitting, emerging happy.

The stuff left in the flue of kills is the substance of actualised life. Here are the actions of life done by the incarnated. Together their substance is a pool of vital content (the tent is actually in a camp) hearty interesting contributions of dopamine that become a means for an idea.

It is not in my interest to be the means for 'human life' but it is interesting to be alive. It is interesting to have the means for life and to revisit the innards of the self as a killer. To kill while stood there and while at it I find new means for life, although as I say life what I mean is linen.

COMIC TIMING

I went to Ilford on my own
walked up a dual carriageway
to McDonalds for a cup of tea and a think then
went back to the clinic with half a blueberry muffin
in my pocket
I was handed a white laminated
square with a number on it
I will be called by the number not
by my name I lied
on the form that asked if there was anyone
at home my Uber arrived
as the cramps started
I was told to be home within one hour
the journey time was 45 minutes
I felt nauseous
breathed slowly
the driver talked about ratings
he liked chatty and punctual passengers
he once gave a married couple no stars
when the man hit the woman
I felt dizzy we drove past his house
that's my house
he looked up my ratings and said I was
above average
you must be a nice person maybe
normally more chatty
I tried to sound lovely
said I was unwell in a weak
voice he joked I would get no stars
if I was sick
I go through my to-do list

to clean an Airbnb
do it for money
I am a bad maid to capital's heart muscle
there was one night between guests
I had a plan to lie down
with the tv on
eat a Marks & Spencer cottage pie
sleep on the sofa wake up
change the bedding
go back to the big cold house I live in and feel
treated
I knew
what to expect from
the last time the pain got
acute on a two-hour arc
I had had a hot bath
I had sat by the bath like a bird
and held
a bundle in my hand
poked about for a god or a plan
what survives a day?
but this time there was no build
up there was no flight
the pain stayed still from the clinic
to the brown
and honourable sofa
not getting easier or worse
I did not
feel anything passing through me
but the room was dark and
around me

I woke up at 7 a.m.
took some painkillers and finished cleaning
I left the key and got the bus
still bleeding a
bit still on the brink
of a big pain but going nowhere
my housemate was having a party
I was very tired but she
is out of sync and soulful
I needed to be dressed and nice
I made a bowl of beetroot
puree and hummus
I made a simple butter pastry
grated cheese
into it twisted the dough into sticks
they snapped in the oven but
smelt delicious for the people
I greeted them alone
didn't know any of them
the pain stayed still I smelt real
leaned on the counter and decided
to drink
some of my friends arrived
I behaved normally
my good friend quietly asked me
to stop being cruel to her
I was very disturbed
told her I didn't feel well
I followed smokers worried about
my good friend's feelings until
I found her in the middle

of some laughing doing
an impression of a cat
scratching a pole

her movements in a black
and white skirt
were comedic
and expert
she moved like a clown she
swung the lower half of her body
left-to-right she upped her arms
stopped to look at the room
through her hair then carried
on clowns invent new grace
for limbs out of ungraceful
lines in the room
I think I was mid verb
like my friend I said to my head
I am mid verb
maybe I have become the verb
I am not having
I am
abortive was the last thing I
thought before falling onto
the purple and habited bed
face down we have to feel
everything in our stomach
ache is tempo
I have seen millions of films
I get it
or there is no story only comedy

but my friend has clowned time
her skirt was so stripy
I am reading it now
a difference between being
scanned for a future
or past material
for latency or tendency
I am very interested in this and I
am interested in the catch of the bed
which idea is homeless?
what is surplus connection to poetry what is the
rushed little examinations on a screen out of view
screened from me the nurse
confirms she can see a vaguer noun
something like a burn
there is not a thing but time read
translated where there might be form
it is there or a picture of noise
not like a construct
of the noise like a head it's this
way up
he is waving
creatively
at the elaborate
so it is just legibility or esoteric
reading styles
the matter
is not interpreted it is agile
easily switches between verb and noun
I could be creative but
I am beginning

to think stuck linguistically
awkward to material or reality
cannot have
have to be
timely nothing has changed
I need to find my friend
the cat the clown so
she can tell me the time
she has animation to give
I went to Ilford alone
was handed a pink laminated square
a staff was inserted I felt
hungry time was coming out slowly
I shouldn't have expected it to happen all at once
but I was told to expect it to happen all at once
they held up the staff
red for someone
I feel like a comedy
that's probably a lot of it there
it's still going on

WELL

as long as you're happy
I don't have to worry

say anything
yes

wrong answer
a stress

yes of course I am
an ancient language
speaking

at a false pair of eyes
like mine
looking
vacant and dumb around and over

the waft around our legs
is going

now look
down on outcomes

o it is me
that account of it is fine
especially the toes

ACT 2

Time for me to resemble my deep shock

When she says I'm dead after falling off her horse, she's not saying it in response to the question, are you hurt? It's not the answer to that question. She would have said it anyway. She says it in the same voice as she swears at the lake. She says it again on her birthday. I am dead. As in, already in death. Actually really fully living a death. Imagine being able to say that? I say it all the time. Holly, this is your appointment date, I'm dead. Holly, you're late, I'm dead. This is your room booking, dead. Happy anniversary, darling, you guessed it. It's the same as when she says when you're a poet, you cannot truly be married. At least you're not in the marriage pro-per-ly. I'd also say, when you're a poet, you're not really at the doctor's, speaking to the strategists, dying. Don't worry I have heard of love. Being a poet being a woman being dead being ecstatic or a cyclist is just as saying I am a poet, I am a woman, I am dead, I am ecstatic and a cyclist. You can say any one of those things about yourself and if you do it is an excellent example of timing. There's no chronology of proof that's relevant to any of them. It's not like saying, I have long hair. It is like saying, in the dream I was dead. That is the voice of accuracy, but now it's hers and now it's mine. Imagine how wonderful it is to speak as wreckage. The timing is incredible. And the oxymoronic completeness of a wreck is . . . I'm still working it out. Maybe after my bath I'll tell you how the voice of a wrecked ship and a woman and a poet in ecstasy cycling are the same. Stop telling me what year it is. Stop telling me what time it is. How old I am.

SHIPBUILDING

prepare the shops will close today
you nod and are licking envelopes in bed
do both

                              the pending breath of withheld action

a unit economic   comes but stopped

                              sits in the middle of a hipbone

          clipboard

                                        humpback

          the soul of a

                                        shopboy

COMMON GRAVES, THE BODY AND THE BLOCKADE

A writer doesn't know where her husband's grave is
has an affair with a gravedigger.

She dreams of him and starts to treat her dreams as places
to understand what prison is.
She meets him at night by drowning in her sleep.

She calls the ritual 'plunging under'

she found his blood in the finished story:
coward   traitor   fascist   a forest

and now my loneliness is a book of him

but The Writers
The writers are on fire

in residence
and preserved

I REACHED A STATE

that body looks outnumbered by erogenous zones
which makes it more or less like a system
of repression or legalised torture
my aspects crush
   I'm wet
his chest is broad and high up – like a TV!
locked my eye and neck

What if men are not church?
our brogues are lifted arms
       cast to running water
so watchem
they instrument my voice
to my sister's to stick hard loot in literature

it's a state
I bang the metal donkey figurine
with a stick
it chimes   I paint his eyes
black with the liquid
boiling between my questions
about his time and weight

BLOOD

My mother told everyone in the village
and at the local art college that she'd die for a blood
velvet cake in the shape of a house. All day I received
and hid progressively larger eventually
life-sized blood cake houses. The art students made the
biggest and most ambitious. It didn't fit in my camera
scope. She can always fake cry. Especially in my camera scope.
The local paper asked how amazed she was.
This is worse than the time she got several abused ponies.
She turned to me and whispered how extremely creepy and
artistic it was for the villagers to do this. The next morning
she lay down on a raft while her anxious friend oared her out to sea.

HAVE DISCOVERED THAT MY MOTHER IS NOT MY REAL MOTHER BUT THE DRUNK WOMAN BANGING ON THE WALL IS

Dinner ruined, I left, embarrassed. Have also found staged pictures of Fake Mother whom I thought until now to be True Mother, holding plastic twins in a birthing pool that is definitely the Jacuzzi in my rich but also imaginary husband's house. She is wearing sunglasses and smiling. I send it to brother with 'suspicious?' noted on back. Eventually find flickering footage of young Fake Mother's training for inauthentic motherhood at the North Laboratory. Girls are strapped to upright tables. Baby alligators dipped in pasta sauce are gaffer taped around their necks. The alligators snap and swing in the hammocks under the girls' chins in order to condition them to care work. Led Zeppelin soundtrack.

TELL THEM I LOVE IT HERE

I don't know how to move again
You know them?
You've met them?
You've heard that they are away travelling?
The heel of my shoe broke
the imbalance caused me to turn around
You know they need me to pay for their roof?
I was lost
tripped and was on the pavement
against it   You'll tell them?
terribly moved   grazed palm bent wrist
both knees in the street
Tell them I love it here
drinking any tiny line of serious life I can
I have one opportunity per day to feel comfortable
and he took it away
he followed me all the way to the station then to the next one
I abandoned all hope of subtle accommodation
Tell them

no drafts or quirked lines this room is about as fine
as a square
just Let me
live here
But the letting is a problem
You are let
It means permit
to Live
she hides
You did let me
I'll get a haircut   It's bleeding now
One day or two more. Negotiate.
There is a purple mark on the side
that wasn't there before
then a nice Mature and silvery pour
out of your estate into pleasure
to cap it all
My ear is green and coming off it hurts to eat

the problem was an old white chair
for an hour I sat on the problem
on the pavement next to a lamp
that heaved up some need to re-do
the movement or is there another way to hold
onto movements
what does the pavement mean by this?   It is modelled
to keep most plans alive . . .
That's my chair
I wobbled and nearly fell
off because
she's right
it is hers
she's staring at it
I'm only sitting on it

THE WORK AND ITS RECORD

You can't separate the work of cutting and gluing the newspaper clippings and organising the meetings and chairing and note taking and making the tea and cataloguing and nursing and protesting and caring and nurturing and washing the cups and booking the busses and decentralising and dismantling power and educating and making the badges and tying the string and folding the box and sending the letters and filing the files and fixing the index and drawing the pamphlets and drawing the logos and listing the agendas and doing the administrative tasks and holding the door open and writing the songs and singing the songs and singing the words bring back my body bring back my body bring back my body to me to the tune of 'My Bonnie Lies Over the Ocean'

and photocopying the songs and saving them and standing in the picket line at Armagh Jail and refusing to strip and refusing to wash and sweeping the floors and linking arms and booking rooms and booking halls and booking meals from the antifascist work from the trade union work from the work of solidarity from the work of working making money to eat from stopping the BNP campaigning outside train stations from blocking Enoch Powell's Unborn Child Protection Bill from licking the stamps and posting the letters and lobbying MPs from making love notes on the back of the envelope from signing on from wishing you well and saying Merry Christmas and writing please call me I cannot pay the telephone from supporting the miners' strike from supporting the steelworkers' struggle from blocking Alton's Bill and blocking the Embryo Bill and blocking Corrie's Bill and the Infant Life Preservation Bill and the Lord Bishop of Birmingham's Embryo Protection Bill from writing the newsletter that says

dear Sisters from booking the May Day stall from singing
Schoolgirls and Secretaries
Schoolgirls and Secretaries working women and wives
Schoolgirls and Secretaries
Schoolgirls and Secretaries working women and wives
from leaving a note that says *look at page 14 it's horrendous*
and reclaiming
the measure of 'survival' from the work of survival
and resisting someone else saying when it is the time of possible
survival and what is the time of possible survival and whose survival
is possible and perceived and
what week of a body of its own weeks does survival start at
from fighting the details of 14 weeks 18 weeks 20 weeks 24 weeks 28
weeks 28 weeks 28 weeks back to 24 weeks from knowing
to survive means what lives next is different
and contains the fight
what survives will not be apart from
what was conceived as she conceived it
what was lived is in what is conceived as survival
what survives is what is prolonged-continued-remade from what was
lived
after and before

life beyond life
is not
made from outside it

the making point of survival can only be attributed to + by she who
has lived

what survives? the work and the tradition of living in the worker
in the records of their songs
the determination is produced from the work done + sung and
cannot be separated from the work of the fight from the work of
asking in the given and perceived moment
who has the right to life?
or from the work of hearing
one song sung to the tune of another's older song

> *Who's got the right to life?*
> *Money buys it*
> *Who's got the right to life?*
> *War denies it*
> *Who's got the right to life?*
> *Those that live it*
> *Who's got the right to life?*
> *We that give it*

A RARE THING TWICE

In my dormition I leave this Iconic city
My hairy saint is here personally
allegoric
will kill
Dormant saint kill! The syntax of fur on fate
is legendary
o legendary!
this is my main strength
it has banged on the window, beds are over
phase two is lying in a pallet
we fell are lethal to uprights
And so go the saints
with hot rude kill

'POETRY AND POVERTY'

for supper a prune bread with sardines

no night
my
Cheery society
dry teats its

Creaturs with esoteric
drills
on artist model life
on a boon in the key of gimmick
monthed
snuggled up to drink
dank beer
poor thing it
in the cup
hollowed out of Life's cold space like
all of the room asks
How often are you sick?

Puss in porch Unconscious – spreads ruin – wake up!
All of the time

ME, POSE? I COULD PAUSE

rat poor we grew up
not far from each other
I have to tell you about a plate of sandwiches
in which your mother is unkilled
fine but you seem to have trapped me in between
some spreadable meat with chutney   my legs
our lives are parting where the knife cuts
the sandwiches found
when she got back from the bunker
on the floor
in the parlour
on the plate but
covered in glass

pause with the bloc   refuse to be seen
stand on my head
sweat (where is my writing about statues?)
not worship
obstinate   persistence of energy
  without life
I think it's called static
like the communard's bone in the wall
          the back of her head ends
pause on produce pose on land
stand on her head

she turned into a statue after all
all I could say was
    we'll have to have under
stood

then resuscitate
sculpt – unsculpt

look down at myself and wonder

is that you
under there like a floor?

you can lagoon
but you cannot not be the floor

you aren't far enough from the firing range

as your guide I should address you more
but I can't get my feelings out
the thought in my head is sustained like the saddest of all students
so I practise each life noise until it's there
the voice that notices everything
a quicker younger screeching
no one should have to choose
between blessings between
being violated or shown
everyone knows the young offenders' institute
(stone quarried by older convicts)
nobody knew that nurses cannot leave the house for five weeks
until all at once each nurse decides to be with other nurses
we cannot cure depression
the campest incubus is the one on top
but I like to be crushed

What seaside is this? What town?

Paul on the sun lounger only has hours. He looked strong, silently ready, with small stars dotted up and down his walnut. Now you see him in the station, nervous, putting spectacles on a peach. It would be inappropriate to remind him how you know each other.

Paul is as confused as a garden

listen with crisis   smelt of limes by the lime wall   plenty of life left

I like the way the toilet bowl faced out diagonally into the bar
there is no need to be perpendicular with the wall for this
unless you don't understand existing patterns
or how to predict the World-Thought
that is coming
then of course you probably would rather stand/sit/buckle
with tradition

The lodge, the changing room. Always put an arch that is always a
tomb in my changing room, please.

Too sharp to go   Too jutting   Like slate, already there

aloneness is so stimulating, too stimulating
It shakes like the wind the tent
an argument of materials
with wilful patches
one day skint
one more like slate
building up a list

this cup feels so full
on the other ride
I fell
tea has deep blisses
is a report on romance
notice all of it
just as much

could you ever imagine a day like this?
not in all my gift shop notebooks

DIP

what were we raised on?
smelly pink and orange dip
the dip is from class
from standing in a fridge glow looking
(want nourishment to feel alive but punished)
in the meantime scoop your finger through four connected tubs
mass mixed dumb resin; a turn; one of potency; a tangy insincere
    blob
constantly hungry   doesn't she feed you?
there's a stiff in the door   knocking for draught
for a suck a soft cry a babe in the base
budget dips   down then up
once angry twice hungry   three to four for a petite movement of
    consciousness
oil the statement abnormal
                I need money to live
stick something in it
(the decadent real)

if you plaster your brags well you-don't-have-to-baroque-yourself

ACT 3

Heavy out there

what's in our cannon *eh*? . . . sugared alcohol . . . lucky drinkers shoot the bin . . . we lace plans for assassins to our cannon . . . the poisonous conditions of seawater *eh*? . . . skin flags and shipping lipids . . . the sea expels cooking fats . . . foul play . . . *ah* . . . animal fingers spread out to massacre . . . a body or a cruet . . . *ah* . . . who is slippery *eh*? . . . a thief or a ghost? . . . this is a risky history . . . less skimmed fat than plan to give up *eh*? . . . who would add wheat . . . *ah* . . . to bread . . . *eh*? to make wet bread pass as dry bread . . . *eh*? add rye or noodles or common semolina . . . you made the bread . . . alcoholic or useful . . . have it to eat . . . or pass us our cannon *eh*? . . . come to the flat . . . give up on food . . . it is very heavy . . . it's not wet . . . just provoking gas in sugar . . . the casual worker eats their conditions . . . if they are . . . *ah* . . . over long *eh*? . . . awkward . . . creative *eh*? . . . like Rosa's ghost story . . . where no one ever swam or got tired . . . *ah* . . . so much for sustenance *eh*? so much for food for all *eh*? We can stomach more than this *ah* . . . body parts are a regular land . . . a crut is a commentary on a crotch and a gut . . . very damp and a dislocated knee . . . *ah* an untreated lump in the other leg . . . swelling is the reason for taking . . . a rest in the café *eh*? . . . the sea is in us and in another shop . . . on the square itself or behind the street lamps and . . . *ah* on the quay . . . fired at . . . sheltered behind the shop . . . continue the fusillade . . . shelter in water . . . the point is we ran . . . slipped . . . there is no plan . . . shoot at . . . my wet friend . . . mushrooms get big on his grave

ECCENTRIC ATTIRE

The attitude of my body is a boy
wearing a cravat
loose around his neck. Fortunately
his passion is easy, it is to be bad
live. That
is something he can do to a candle
wick and still be on either side

of an appearance. He reasons,
when wearing a cravat, that
he is on both sides
of a silky scarf

so he can exceed
the limits of silky, neatly
with an eloquent kick of
the whole of Cinema,
two hot cups and Jason
holding something heavy
in his antler.

He must telephone his friends.
He calls them, is my body silky?
is this live?
Surely the throat is a neurone?

He hangs up. They visit him in the salon of a
pretend theatre. Wednesday, feeble.

By undoing the knot around their bad
friend's neck they
feel close to him, the session, they tremble
at another body near.

It is an Eiffel Tower, a Shakespeare, a criminal
happiness unfurls in front
of them. Tiny scarlet trout crawl out.

How his friends wish they could know him like
that. By a slack knot of scarf the boy was stylish.

He turned
to his friends, and with the attitude of a boy
said, I want passionate stories that knot and ruffle, let the ends hang
out, let Cinema and Europa and Confession end now,
different patterned will.

They were affectionate where they met to discuss
the avant-garde rules to suffering
gone are powders, supple and how to dash.

The friends disappear. The boy loosely exists as a style.

A boy barely understands it exists. He thinks
its act is its life. Craves mountain postcards,
the fiery pleasure of learning to swim
become a pedal
wheeled in.

My boy works hard to exist.
It senses an injury and has to feel its way back
into a state of mass injury.

To feel its gore, to feel bombardier, it finds a story to be with.
My boy is a body of troubled water. A swashbuckler. The dancer. Maid.

Neither has ever been in such a state. The boy reaches
to the bar. This is how it is discovered, by its loud, reluctant pose.

My body has an industry in that boy, it contrives
a life. The way the boy flinches and reacts
is a coordination of the way my body loves to will
itself a little destroyed.

My boy is a satire
a dumbshow accident.

ARE YOU WRITING ABOUT LOVE?

No farming practices
O the industry around love
If we diversify our farming we will manoeuvre
our love out of the desert
Different types of dairy?
Different beasts and handlings of beasts will produce new love
Love has always moved with farming
Yes love has always moved forward with farming
Every sexuality has a knowledge and technology and every new way
to move beasts from one crate to another produces a metaphor
distinct to a loving gesture rooted in historical economic
packed-full machines –
methods for milking and experimental love poems or cheese

THE END SMELL WHERE ENGLISH DIED

on the altered face of an abusive moon
pain feels like the fault of them in pain
local and inevitable
frilled collateral shapes with anguish.

Abuse is the conjuring of madness
outside of yours in the nursery of another
an abusive relation makes you immediately difficult
got soft lumps on it   the substrates of an emotional abuser have
    turned contradictive   they've gone into a shell call into the shell
this is breached relationality
there is no tool but what you're doing is abusive
dig your hand into the shell
pull out soft lumps there are lumps and there are abusers
the abused dig into their past to pull out their lumps.

Here comes my abuser now in through the patio door
he silently passes   he's still
on the phone
I press myself against the blue rolled-up mat by the wall
now life lumps are gone
or like a set I can still celebrate the lumps of life the moon is beautiful
    I stuck my hand in it   pulled out soft lumps the moon is a lump
no the moon is abusive   it applied for a job
settled down in the rest of the sea to think
I thought this was a wish but this is not a wish this is
the End Smell Where English Died.

BOG BUTTER

is a dairy product, churned from the cream of animal milk. It is found buried in peat bogs in a wooden keg or as a massive unclothed lump. It could be used to pay the rent or rested next to the sick. If the patient died the butter had to be buried. Butter is the richest and most delicious food.

Some bog butter found in Irish bogs dates back to the first century AD. Fifty kilos of butter found in Tullamore, County Offaly was buried five thousand years ago. When it was opened the archaeologist said it smelt buttery.

Sinking butter into the bogs has a practical and symbolic logic. Votive butter burials were offered to the territorial and fertility gods. The earth goddess guards the sacred office of the king because of the butter. The bog shores up the sovereignty of the king. This king is the body of the land. This butter moves from the produce of daylight to a system of economy in the underworld.

The butter churns were put into the ground next to bog bodies. Bog bodies are the human version of butter. They were either political prisoners offered to the gods or they were themselves sacked kings. The Old Croghan Man was tall and beautiful. He had to be dismembered, his nipples cut off, his thorax had to be threaded out. His subjects can never suck his nipples.

Excavated bog people often have intestines loaded with perfectly preserved ceremonial meals composed of cereals, buttermilk, barley and locally found seeds. The body takes a bellyful of food into the bog to the gods.

The remarkable preservation is because of the acid, it's because of the lack of oxygen, it's because of the sphagnum moss.

Burial is also a practical method of preserving foodstuffs or sacramental insurance for more food and more butter. A churn's burial conserves it in the peat and ensures the health of the unburied one. It's a purchase. Burying it means thousands of years later, since before the time of Christ, it still smells buttery. The fermentation process is in collaboration with microbes, bringing out delicious new flavours. Burying it also makes it disappear. The butter becomes meaningful but invisible, in the psyche of the soil. Burial shores up a subject on top, like the latent dream of a territory.

IT WAS A HOT PATIO

Moneybags asleep on your knee
you said burning but you were sweating
I went inside to eat
quivered because it's self-consciously
like memory to enjoy soup
       but slurped Dad's lip
and called back 'I sanded the furniture'
you were still alone in the garden
'you can sell it now'
no response
honestly
a man could get rich from all the stopped
hearts that ought to beat
on a Monday
inside an August

ACTIONS AND APPETITES; GEOMETRY, SURFACES AND SOLIDS

An Idea comes along that is so adequate it must belong to God
My friends watched me take the hot-based cup
from someone else's table and drink it   I welled with spirit
a crushed seed drink that was thick as passage mush   so I used a
    spoon. They planned and watched but I was the one   a hit in the
    world   who took the cup   I was the one
who drank it
Milled pips and another huge starch   digesting all the time when on
    the continent. Eventualising some composite
of rogue measures on a bar stool.
It was the Thursday of self-reflection. Afterwards
a roaring sound   There was only just time to think it through   raise
    the cup say,
To adventure! Down it, damn a few souls.
The ego of a plan classed the outfit
that was a chunky thought turned throat-butt
    The effects never wore off
not the protonate drink nor
the idea to steal it
There were fifteen artists in the room
for freedom there was a sexed motorbike gang
but I was the one who drank it I was the one whose tongue swelled

HOW AND WHY TO MAKE PORRIDGE

because you like to venture beyond
without moving and grains bloat in milk
porridge is a real meal ancient and coming
composed like courage in a long rough
minute of nettles and chamomile seeds
Yorkshire fog seed   knotweed hen sick
buckwheat   spit clag store mumps
pike dumplings herb-spiked
then the worst soldier had my foot halted said
hey martyr hey suckling keep
for all the time spent softening
you're full
forthcoming you're funk
I said I'm heavy sauce myth-bulked
a cup of roux
I am cope pod definitely a shape
lying on birth soap
hoping for mercy or myrtle
for a truant to turn out the future
fully preserved and
unworrying cheese in the rot cupboard
but O no – I am turning into someone's artisanal idea!
I am for the farm shop expensive
was bled relaxed and led to a peat pit
a blindfold braided into my hair
drawn and packed down belly taped
jaw swapped for an older
masculine shoulder joint
still and sensitive for centuries
since I am on the telephone waiting
for the opening times to your museum

A TOO TINY SPACE OF LUCENT WORLD BUT HORRIFY ME

there'll be bruises and examples of England – for inertia – an appetite I will lie down – my mother is here – I am buying a new tent – she is obsessed with the weight of it – convinced it will topple me – off my bike – the vision of me from behind makes us both laugh – slowly and into a hedge – she has never – as far as I can remember – wondered what weight – I can bear – for how long – I can lift her up – she makes me wear the bag in the shop – she nudges me – I push her back – you'll never make it – I hear her say – buying a tent is unnatural – but as I explained – to her afterwards in the café – on my lap the tent – bouncing in between our faces – I have to fling – myself – into stupid habitations – to feel at least a little – chic ethic – snug in grand unearthings – of raw perspective – she jabs me awake – with her spoon – I have sage oil on my wrists – pills for concentration

THE NIGHT'S PUTATIVE UNION

we go alone at night down
low light the house with a switch
one hand is moving itself
to tea on the shelf
elements not got down without climbing
bad us turning
half pinched a life
all mighty
comfort to women admiring
their self-haunted intimacy
we are together
we cub the hole
routing resources
to crab-crawl out of the bun into morning
into the scandalous version of weekdays
my thin legal personality
emerges from this
the gist of sleep
this puffy impish face
looks up when everyone agrees
it pushes my beliefs out like eyeballs
sucks experience in with a tongue
sing to the morals the undoing clicks
we talk about pork fat
the moral is distributed
everyone agreed

(TIRED)

My mentor is advising me to advance my form by trimming the
thoughts off a child
to learn from their Behavioural Escape   I have her by the window
am taking notes
you blink a lot
yes I'm trying to invert this exchange
what else
the University
the wishbone in the corpus of my University
      I am caught
not only leaning against the toilet wall
but facing the wall and spread against it
Susan asks if you're ok
Susan's trousers are very nice
She has to go she has words swimming in her head
On the stairs maybe you'll see Susan again
Compare the behaviour of the voice in your head when it creates lists
to when it creates clauses   does it sound tired?
this might be it registering content or it may be designing a thought
to say something careerist

SLEEPING BAG

people buy a house
they think they are a family
but they are a car
they are
a soft moan at night
the sleeping bag is a singlet
it is warm
the wearer feels vermiformed and Soviet
heat heats them
like the circulation of rights
to buy or to heat
to the life of my life
it has a graph up the side
descending extremes
I'm lying
inside the bag all the time
my watery eye wets
the fabric to a nylon slime
when I peak at the sunrise through two
tent doors
it might be a theatre
that's eccentric to the farmer
I cute
survival mime artiste
scaled & speaking to nature
as model coma
now everyone is intrepid and Mars-themed
they think they are alive but
they are in a campsite shop
when it's over
I want to see a production line of sleeping bags

ACT 4

1st person (heartbroken) wanting hoping fearing that
2nd person (heartbroken) does something

To get to the library I have to walk 15 minutes along Seven Sisters Road to the underground stop, sit on the tube for 15 minutes without much air, then walk for 5 minutes along Euston Road. These roads are two of the most polluted roads in London, the most polluted city in Europe. When I get to the library I have swallowed so much toxic air my lungs ache, my eyes are yellow, my teeth crunch, my head stings. I get my books and read about port towns and I buzz remembering what I'm being charged to sit here. My eyes are yellow. I see cars and boats fighting. I imagine it as something going on between my legs.

HANNAH WEINER'S SINK

Somewhere in San Diego, under a flight path, there is a bungalow that you can reach by train from Los Angeles. I travelled there to sleep and read. On the third day I cried as she described her decision to live in the kitchen sink.

a space to both urinate and drink without moving
a bay to

study herself

The men I stayed with offered me ear plugs and told me to look out for the seals from the bus window. I got off the bus and walked right up to them. I went back to the library and got in the sink with her.

To pee on the burns on her toes
I agreed. Caught myself
regarding one perspective from another, nodding
she got in the sink   the sink is a fixing point of institution &
hallucination.   There we were in the sink too; good idea.
For three weeks

The librarian explained. The shower's flow was inadequate; pouring water onto body parts eased pain. The shower was metal and she had become magnetic, the sink was ceramic. She didn't have a bathtub.

Back in my room I chewed. I could hear the errors. The communal curve of her visions centred in the sink. A small dog sat on the edge. The sink is a state. Making statements in the Sink – of the drain? – means you are not opposed to will – everything you write from here addresses faith in utensils   time is done

It's time to get up have a shower, pack a bag for the day, link things. It's cold in the reading rooms. Seals. Nothing until   she's still in the sink

Being in the sink makes you different to the rules of the home – it's a new way to be at home (in self, in body – yes it's trial by error).

Let's think of the woman in art history, sitting at her toilette. We are behind her, she has her arm raised and is lancing her era's attitude towards us from her nipple in inches and its niches   This is a version of that she found an experimental position   she found a space to recover   to make looking for her

The sink is a space of not-yet and cure
burning little moons onto her breast
a thing done to meaning and my love of this
underneath-knowledge

inventive. I lay down along a route of study.

Her writing is in colour-coded pens. I learnt the language of her
paranoia: red, green, purple, there is a purple man at the door
don't answer it the librarian disagrees we are not speaking

Language transformed toes, it was in her hair, the scratching of cloth
on skin, as pain or thirst. Language like water in a hole.

my hero is starving
I am reading

I did dry her hands
I do have
a spiritual convention
the energy
the luxury
I am begging to hold her paper
the sink in the place of arthritic pain

I was in the country   aren't I?
peeing in it   washing it off   having time to think
I got in the sink didn't I?

SEX WITH LODGERS

What will we tell our bosses?

Tilts the jar of dog biscuits
Considers subsistence

What did you rescue
from the marriage?
Sex with lodgers

You don't pay me enough
Cut yourself up

Construct a public from which flatmates use plastic razors, from who
sees themselves in civilisation, from who finds they are spent
who used cream

We have an exfoliation mitt each to rub the ridiculous sadness on
everything
8 rooms 8 shampoos an archaeology

Excuse me

I am trying to write poetry into my age, the specific time of my body
and the life it does but the age of the planet but that's the point

Poor you,
are you shocked by the sound of another's laundry

PRAYER

Can someone else help my friend breathe through
her panic attack? my face is too funny
if I count I return
I fell in those bins? You got in, you were fine –
you just got in

I hope I can trust my friends' therapists
after a break here is hard skin   she walks away
look after her   her healthy reasons spike out the back of her shirt
    look after her
I hope therapy is real I hope it's healthy   it is expensive
pair up talent and mutilate
whose little bench can version memory   and who likes my lamb now
it's a known conductor

On a guided tour of a life-size doll factory they offered me a freebie to
take home.
In bed it transformed into a violent and abusive husband.

Working together since 1998 working together since 2010
throw confetti down the stairwell

WHO IN THEIR HANGING SAC

home
a natural oven

work
a natural fridge
an intense stare learnt in childhood

a logic of Me like a glowing white ball
becomes dislodged from a pocket or
a jar that every hour on the hour
I have to grumpily lean out of bed and stir

years later on the phone to Em, *you do it too?*
she says, it's an accession into being from inside out that drafts self
a natural church

lean with your heart
you r ignored

years later
in the park with dialogue –
that's a big goat
yes, it is a big goat
it's a donkey
you always do this
in the meantime, my poor ceremonial trellis table collapses
loneliness is a love story
of time and headspace
and the present?
this is why we cannot feel it
having a bath in nature is not a state within a state, it is all bath time

what are you having?
only the same oceanic feeling

      same day
will I ever shave my Bambi again?
will I ever give a rat?
stare down at my sausages then up at my friend
give up
obnoxious
      that evening
undress
have a fight with ideas
whether the soft emanations of livelihood
are mucus or revelatory
alone still

      evening again days later
feel the muscles in your > are they tight?
no yes (laughter) maybe
try again
admit that you are here and have paid
there that's better
good idea!

      days later
where in my head is Fashion? maybe scripture, pulses of afterlife
just clumped expressions
you should feel annotated by this
it's indeterminacy that drives us mad then again therapeutic hitting
hurts like it's your mum doing it

INTERNATIONAL WORKERS' DAY

I was put into a rare recovery position
the shape of bog people in loose rope
My niece sings a song under her fleece
he only had to peep in, to peep in, but he still couldn't do it
I hand her two lions to put in her cheeks, purple and yellow
There's too much to do around here
What is wrong with her?
they're pointing at my earring
Someone is very small she's crawling over my knees and whispering
to her brother, why did she come here? You cannot move, you mean
something else
Not your plot, particular dirt, the plot, its expressive stillness
She fell and slapped her head on my laptop
\, 5   name the poem, devotional shipwreck
Women lie down in various rooms of the house
taken in by an older brother's homeopathic handling
edged up to the dinner table
Glasses in memory of running somewhere else with socks on,
she's on the kitchen floor
The kitchen floor?
This is the seabed, a melted spine, proto-storytelling
Use the swan-necked-spider to get over an obstructing ball
No problem, you guys look great together, I'll just dissolve
This avenue gets more political every time I walk it
William Blake never left town
A man with a gentle northern voice shouts with real excitement, *Has
it nestled?*
Has it nestled? It has
it's soaking

DIGS

For water for tea go to the well

winch the chain
look at where the bucket dropped
it fled my heart for water

We still live in an old school.

There were forewarnings of other worlds coming and colossal
alterations

The children are gone
but there are jars of pickle
herbs drying on the beds
little urinals, a poster that demonstrates a shepherd
pots of sacred basil in the cabinet

The building stands
we stand in a queue for tampons
and have eaten generous food like knödel
speak slowly in a range of accents about our projects
Everyone exchanges products some techniques
we should worry and cloak
I zone out
the apothecary is German the prison diary on the shelf
is in German

The well is next to the public library
the library is a small house with lace curtains
Society desires itself doesn't it, bucket?
Civic spaces find each other, don't they?
Like timely comrades gone pretty for a public that can never find
them

The bucket fills the bottles
I've been drinking well-water since the 90s to make my chest and
books fuller to make my organs tougher for examination or the kind
of contact where
one body offsets another
to be replenished
We want to be on track, remembered
The winched arm said, Hello friend, hello no one

The student says there's a weed that grows everywhere and it's edible,
I say OK
I'll just eat that then, I'll go and pull up a handful whenever I'm
hungry

the singer shifts
but for the sake of medievalism make an appointment with the bread
woman
she'll leave it on the stone in case you bring bad news
Let the man in the shop stand alone

We are living to imagine.

It feels casual and anxious, I can't pretend to know where the car is or
what it's for but Gabby drives and Armine drives and the actor drives

There are wish structures to train along,
plant things, invent songs

practise saying, this house and this way
this is what we do

Know your job
take the compost to the stinky shed
in sync with utopia and not just tasks
but suck off
the salt soil, stave off the rot in our root
We might rescue the plot with miniature work
expressions of eco-gothic in the hand soap
or call the old bucket a love

shell me
Everyone is preserving
fermenting radish leaves, reducing it, doing a brew
something from dill
I am downloading boxing movies it is similar
it's about turning up and cutting your eyelid, praying
now you can see

Winding our ideas to the community
because a bag of cherries
gets less and less satisfying
Today feels like a territory stupidly reclaimed
also romantic
in my grey fast running suit

I can see enough through the bled-out swelling to put
down the bucket
it goes next to where a child has scratched
'Hanging Out! 1986' and a large dead wasp
the student thinks it's a new hornet
your tincture must be the 80s returning
I hope it won't work

At the well I should've sang
everything echoes, I can see a factory
and I pray in the shower
we are getting close to something

We still live in an old brothel.

we are here to brace the building's shared space
but the dressmaker sat in a cloth chair describing bluebells
puked up then gave them a deadline
adding something to her skin, hustled details of publics
Spring with bliss it came in bluebells
I bring a sweet to her bath
she has shell lacquer placemats to eat off
and the light is so pink in her kitchen

the beer can spits
I am under a blanket but can see the subtitles through a hole
so we talk
follow the story then lose it

Someone arrives with a packet, I don't eat
just listen to their mouths and can see
Maggie's through the hole

everyone is gasping for air

We still live in an old coach house.

through the window horned sheep turn around very slowly
to suggest death
I lie back down, always tired, and saying it
we are lifted, trollied, spread on one patch of mattress
then on another

Like a pen I roll over to face a strange torso
it asks me to think of lungs
I imagine two boots full of water that leak
That's the liquid of the imminent, says the bucket

The future tense is dumb
a dormant sparrow confused

This apartment to live in lives on
which is where you found the mop
a comedian and a living

You have to like it here enough to give the fire a brick of turf, our
hands smell of it
our throats are pinched, it is sweet like modernity's bile

The house is a gang of untalented men
a ruff in charge of its head with pipes
ginning fibres greening aloneness
buff in a furnace, all bondage
I leave the house, my leg
to bed go in it and go out
It's time to tend to something bigger than us
progress in a suite of habits
stink the pig
A century in the marsh and a lizard shit
Something nested there, can you see it?
On imaginary cotton
you can make things with it

cling on
to each other
in a hall

We still live in an old hotel.

no body wants to leave unless it gets lighter
the owner has a nineteenth-century ambition that is madness
she has made marmalade
bowed hope

a young mum orgasms through the ceiling
Don't be happy with nearness, urge on in steps to something else
in very convincing stages followed by a miraculous twist ending
like the Industrial Revolution and since
or the death of punk and since

we are communally apologetic
it's just a bucket
bohemians sleep in digs they
are the works' fancy pragmatism
I'm listening

the bucket said, dig
this is where you live

make plans
or drop
optimistic quenelles, a loaf

VILLETTE

In the novel *Villette*, either I or Lucy Snowe live and work in a girls' school that either she or I found in a small French town. She has nowhere / I have nowhere and no thing in which to hide any of her few / my few possessions. Her mattresses / my mattresses and bedding in the dormitory where she sleeps / I sleep are checked over daily, and she suspects / I suspect that her / my desk in the classroom is also looked through.

She has nowhere / I have nowhere to hide a letter that was sent to her / to me by Dr Graham, who she has a heavy and imaginative crush on / who I have a heavy and imaginative crush on.

She invests / I invest in the letter a devotional adoration that mismatches the friendly goodwill it was written with.

I / Lucy guess that the schoolmistress has snatched, read and then returned the letter to under her / my bed. Lucy panics over her / my lack of private space and makes the eccentric decision to bury the letter in the garden grounds of the school.

She folds the pages tightly / I fold the pages tightly, wrap them in a silk handkerchief dipped in oil, curl them into a glass bottle and hermetically seal the bottle with wax.

She buries the bottle / I bury the bottle under the roots of an ivy bush in an area of the garden that is haunted by either me or the ghost of a nun who was buried alive.

In this gesture / in my gesture, Lucy Snowe rejects the possibility of possessing the letter. She applies / I apply a fantastical value to the letter. The letter passes into an earthed state of absence. I use / Lucy uses burial as a way to disown the letter and to refuse being privately subjected by the letter. She instead / I instead ecstatically ritualise her poverty / my poverty, and her otherness / my otherness to ownership of objects, and evacuate the self into love.

Heavy ending

A great aunt, a dangerously ill alcoholic, is in a hotel room. It is very 1960s. Her exasperated husband is sitting next to her on the bed. He is saying to her that he cannot go on; that he will leave if she doesn't stop drinking. He leaves the room. The great aunt does a calculation: she cannot stop drinking, she cannot live without him, and so she cannot go on. She climbs onto the window ledge and is balancing on the cusp when her husband comes back into the room to say he is sorry, he will never leave. She turns to see him and falls.

Uncus basic of uncus

slap on slap

turned plank

procreative topic

Stupid

Stupa

a body part

you really held the room

I mean you really

held the room

ACKNOWLEDGEMENTS

'Thirty-six' quotes a poem by Marilyn Monroe, *Fragments: Poems, Intimate Notes, Letters by Marilyn Monroe*, ed. Stanley Buchthal and Bernard Comment (London: HarperCollins, 2010), p. 73, quoted in *Women in Dark Times*, Jacqueline Rose (London: Bloomsbury Press, 2014), p. 128.

'Doctor!' uses materials from *Silas Marner* by George Eliot.

The second line in 'Aborted' quotes William Blake's *America a Prophecy*.

'Common Graves . . .' references *Going Under* by Lydia Chukovskaya, trans. Peter M. Weston (London: Barrie & Jenkins, 1972).

'The Work and its Record' quotes from a 1980s National Abortion Campaign protest song sheet found in archives held at Glasgow Women's Library.

'Me, Pose? I Could Pause' quotes a line from *Sans toit ni loi / Vagabond* by Agnès Varda, 1985, as its title.

'Hannah Weiner's Sink' uses research notes made from the Hannah Weiner Papers held at University of California, San Diego.

Early and other versions of some poems printed here have appeared in *Datableed*, *Fandom as Methodology* (Goldsmiths Press, 2019), *Firewall*, Freelands Foundation (catalogue, 2019), *Granta*, *Pain*, *Pelt*, *Poetry Review*, *Repeal the 8th Anthology* (Sad Press, 2018), *Shitwonder*. Thank you to the editors of these spaces for their feedback and community. I am eternally grateful to and amazed by Rachael Allen's editorial courage and care. I am indebted to writers whose combination of friendship, influence and collaboration inspires and creates all of this work. The bird a nest, the spider a web . . .

I owe a special thanks to Eileen O'Hanlon of Clonearl for letting me sleep in her house for a week in 2018.